W9-DDG-135

Your
Magnificent
Declaration

Your

Magnificent Declaration

by

Bruce Allyn Findlay
Esther Blair Findlay

Illustrated by
Bill Dove

HOLT, RINEHART AND WINSTON, INC., NEW YORK

ABOUT THE AUTHORS

BRUCE ALLYN FINDLAY is a former Associate Superintendent of the Los Angeles City Public Schools, and author of Guaranteed For Life. *Together with his wife ESTHER BLAIR FIND-LAY he has also written* Your Rugged Constitution *and other books.*

CONTENTS

The Declaration
of Independence

Modern civilization floats on oil. Oil is nearly as necessary to our way of living as the air we breathe and the food we eat. Imagine how your daily life would change were there no oil. Agriculture, the arts, business, commerce, communication, education, industry, the professions, trade, transportation, and all the interests that grow from them, would slow to a snail's pace. The flame in the torch of liberty itself would dim to a flicker.

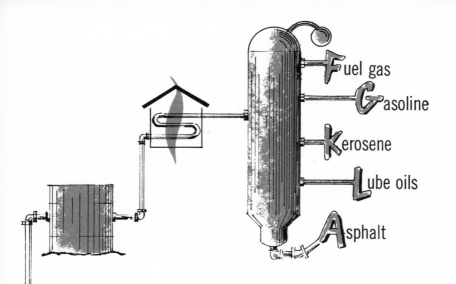

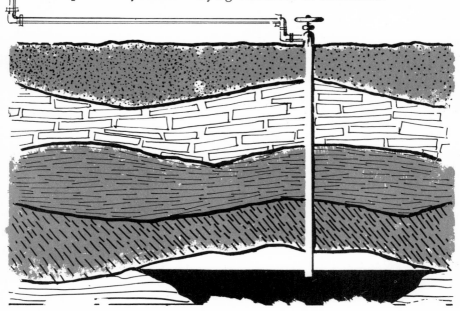

When a drop of crude oil is brought to the surface of the earth and is sent to the refinery, the drop may turn into many products ranging from asphalt to fuel gas. What the crude oil will finally become is determined in the refining process. There are within each drop of crude oil certain natural or "unalienable" characteristics that enable the drop to perform in specific ways under varying conditions of refinement.

Oil has been well called "buried sunlight." Millions of years ago, as they do today, living plants, sea, and animal life got their energy from the light and heat of the sun. In the test tube of nature this organic matter was changed into oil, retaining within itself the energy of the sun.

Through eons of time the oil deposits remained covered by sand and rocks. Man, by hard, intelligent effort, brings this oil to the surface.

There is a similarity between crude oil and Liberty. Each has within itself remarkable powers put there by the Creator. When refined by the processes of experience, Liberty produces forces that have changed and can change men's lives.

As drops of oil may be transformed into more than 2,000 products, so may free men in an atmosphere of Liberty develop limitless capacities.

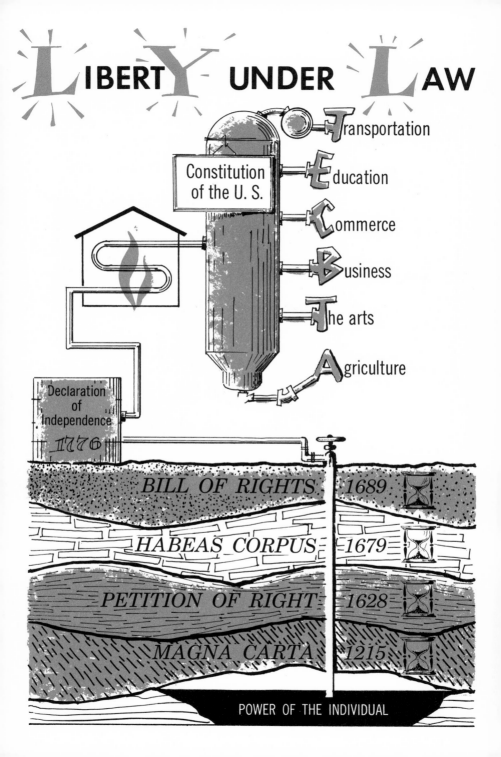

Deep in the Sands of Time "Nature's God" placed Liberty, the buried sunlight of self-government. There Liberty remained waiting, waiting for men to discover it. Some of it seeped to the surface in small amounts and was put to limited uses. To secure it in large amounts, however, men had to dig for Liberty, then refine it and put it to use in brightening their paths and making their lives more livable, enjoyable, and useful.

In you are certain "unalienable rights," powers that belong to you; powers not given to you by kings, potentates, or legislatures; powers which are a part of you; powers which your ancestors spent centuries discovering and refining. Today these powers are harnessed for your social, religious, economic, and political advancement. However, unless this priceless treasure is carefully guarded by each generation, it can be lost forever. Protect and cherish your freedom. Once it is surrendered you may never regain it!

Your "unalienable rights" make each citizen important. They make government your tool and not your master. They make your government one *of laws;* not of men. These facts are of the utmost importance. They are the main difference between representative governments and dictatorships.

All of your powers are buried in the word LIBERTY— Liberty, which is stored deep in the hearts of men, placed there by the Creator, just as He placed latent power in the heart of each tiny drop of crude oil.

The individual drop of crude oil is of little value by itself, and yet within that drop are powers which, when combined with millions of other drops can produce a tremendous force. Just as crude oil is collected in tanks to await refining, so Thomas Jefferson and his associates gathered into the Declaration of Independence the forces of Liberty that had been working their way up through the Sands of Time to the year 1776.

When these forces were accumulated in the Declaration of Independence and refined through the Constitution of the United States, there was brought into being a new power of self-government never before equaled in history. That power is your government, and *YOU* are a vital, dynamic part of it.

11

Magna Carta—the Great Charter of England—was the first stratum, or layer, of the Sands of Time through which modern self-government passed as it emerged from the darkness of tyranny. Much of the language of Magna Carta is strange, because it deals with situations which no longer exist. It does not have a great deal to do with democracy as *you* practice it. However, the fact that Magna Carta was granted is of great importance to you.

The Great Charter was originally intended primarily for the benefit of the nobility. But the restrictions it placed on the monarchy served as a protection for all the people. Each king of England after John agreed to obey its terms. Some of them did so and others promptly forgot or disregarded their promises. The fact that many kings after John accepted Magna Carta did much to establish *your* civil rights. Years later, when the people of England were having trouble with the kings who were tyrants, the people would point to Magna Carta and remind the kings that they had no right to take away the liberties guaranteed in it.

A few of the important matters discussed in Magna Carta include debts, reforms of the courts, abuses of local governments, unfair taxation, imprisonment without trial, taking of private lands, and other problems that were bothering the people in the year 1215.

Some Englishmen have called Magna Carta their Declaration of Independence. Magna Carta is one of the four major secular influences that are reflected in your Declaration of Independence. The other three are the Petition of Right, the Habeas Corpus Act, and the English Bill of Rights. Each of these marked a step toward the freedom and Liberty you now enjoy.

The Petition of Right was the second stratum of the Sands of Time through which self-government passed in its long journey upwards from tyranny to the sunlight of freedom.

About the time the colonists were first settling in America, a new struggle for Liberty was under way in England. This contest was precipitated by a stubborn king, Charles I, who wanted to rule without interference. But the members of Parliament were determined to limit the king's authority, and they refused to grant the funds he needed to carry on his government. Finally on June 7, 1628, Charles I, with no intention of keeping his word, signed a Petition of Right which the members of Parliament had drawn up. This document was basically a demand that the king admit that the people had certain rights which he had disregarded.

Petition of Right dealt with four main grievances. The king was prohibited from:

(1) Forcing people to lend money;

(2) Throwing people into prison without a just cause;

(3) Requiring people to take soldiers into their homes;

(4) Enforcing military laws in time of peace.

The next important milestone in the Sands of Time was marked by the Habeas Corpus Act, which provided further safeguards against abuse of royal authority. One of the king's favorite ways of eliminating critics or political enemies was to throw them into jail. Often he did this without bringing charges against the jailed persons or bringing them to trial. This method of dealing with political opposition is practiced *today* in countries where dictators rule.

14

After much abuse of the rights of individuals, the English Parliament on May 26, 1679, passed the Habeas Corpus Act. The words *Habeas Corpus* are Latin words which mean that a person must be brought before a court or a judge. When the accused person was brought into court, the judge would then decide whether he should be held for trial or set free.

The principle of Habeas Corpus did not originate in 1679. It dates back hundreds of years to a principle found in Magna Carta and also reflected in the Petition of Right. But often the right of Habeas Corpus was ignored or abused by tyran-

nical kings or their officials. The Habeas Corpus Act is important because it forced royal officers and judges, under threat of heavy penalty, to grant a speedy hearing to accused persons and to release them if they could not be formally charged with wrong doing.

The process of bringing men's liberties to the surface where they could be collected and defined in your Declaration of Independence was not completed with the Habeas Corpus Act. One more tyrannical king, James II, had to be overthrown. His actions caused a revolt in England and resulted in the king's daughter, Mary, and her husband, William of Orange, being offered the throne. Determined to have no repetition of abuses of former kings, Parliament passed the now famous Bill of Rights on December 16, 1689. Upon this English document is patterned our federal Bill of Rights and our fifty State bills of rights.

BILL OF RIGHTS · 1689

The English Bill of Rights did not introduce any new principles into English law. Rather it summarized and clarified the rights of the people so there could be no doubt about them in the minds of either the king or his subjects.

The main provisions included:

(1) Forbidding courts to inflict cruel and unjust punishment;

(2) Forbidding excessive bail or fines;

(3) Giving Parliament unlimited and unrestricted freedom of speech in all debates and sessions;

(4) Forbidding the king to levy taxes or maintain standing armies without the consent of Parliament;

(5) Providing that the people might petition the king if and when they felt they had a grievance.

Sometimes earthquakes and other forces cause the pipe, through which crude oil is brought to the surface, to break. The flow is stopped and at considerable cost the break is repaired. This is true of freedom also. Its flow up through the Sands of Time has not been steady and uninterrupted. There have been many breaks which have had to be mended at great personal sacrifice and cost in lives and liberties.

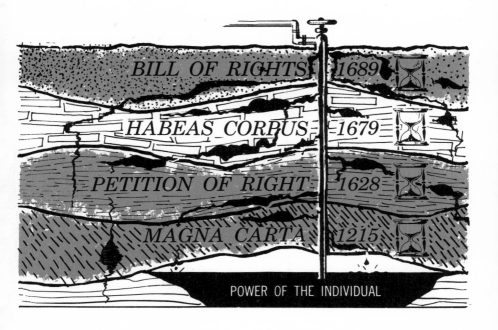

BILL OF RIGHTS 1689

HABEAS CORPUS 1679

PETITION OF RIGHT 1628

MAGNA CARTA 1215

POWER OF THE INDIVIDUAL

There are many lands today where this precious commodity—Liberty—no longer exists.

Unless you guard *your* liberties, you, too, can lose them.

★ ★ ★

The Declaration of Independence was the outgrowth of a series of abuses which the British king and Parliament heaped on the colonists. Most of these abuses were forbidden by law in England. Because the colonists regarded themselves basically as Englishmen living under English laws, they were embittered by the acts of the king and his governors—acts which would never have been forced on the people in England.

Many of the colonists sought only relief from the oppressive acts; independence was in the minds of a minority. When, however, repeated pleas for relief were ignored, and added offenses were the answer to requests for consideration, public sentiment for independence grew rapidly. Colonial leaders decided to do something about it.

The Continental Congress appointed a committee to put in writing the feelings of the colonists. This document was to list the grievances and abuses of the British king and Parliament, and at the same time declare the Colonies independent of Britain.

The committee consisted of Thomas Jefferson, Benjamin Franklin, John Adams, Roger Sherman, and Robert Livingston. Jefferson was asked to be the principal author. He has been called the architect of the Declaration of Independence. At the time, Jefferson was not well known, except in his local community and state. He was thirty-three years of age. He had written, anonymously, a widely read pamphlet titled, "A Summary View of the Rights of British America." The pamphlet had excited the imagination and interest of thousands who did not know its author. Because of this work and his background, Jefferson was considered best prepared to draft the Declaration of Independence. Jefferson was a highly educated man who was acquainted with the governments of other lands and times, and with the writings of the leading political philosophers.

There stands today on the southwest corner of Market and Seventh Streets in Philadelphia, Pennsylvania, adjoining the Mall in front of Independence Square, a tablet that marks the location of the old Graff House where Jefferson wrote the Declaration.

Jefferson's aim was to state in clear, logical, understandable language the cause of the colonists. He wanted it to be a reflection, in sharp focus, of American thinking. He later said that he had not copied from any of his other writings in drafting the Declaration.

So thoroughly did Jefferson cover the ground that much of the Constitution can be traced directly or indirectly to the Declaration. The Constitution seems to have been written with the Declaration spread before its authors.

Jefferson drew generously on his gift of expression and on his knowledge of history to give to the world a statement of the "unalienable" right of free men to remain free. His is a statement of liberty-loving people everywhere of their God-given, not state-given, rights to "life, liberty and the pursuit of happiness."

The Declaration outlines no pattern of government, no code or creed of human behavior, or platforms for men to abide by. It makes no claim to a solution of the political, social, or economic ills of Jefferson's or our age.

It does, however, in crystal-clear, understandable, almost poetic language, present the case of the most humble, or the mightiest citizen in his quest for freedom and liberty—both for himself and for his children's children.

The Declaration after being signed was given into the care of President Washington and later, in accordance with an act of September 15, 1789, to the custody of the Department of State. When the capture of the city of Washington by the British in 1814 was imminent, the Secretary of State, James Monroe, was able to remove it and all of the other state papers to a safe place.

The original Declaration of Independence was exhibited for many years until light and air threatened its destruction. On September 29, 1921, it was transferred to the Library of Congress and placed in a special shrine that prevents deterioration. Every visitor to Washington should see it.

When the fifty-six signers wrote their names at the bottom of the Declaration some of them knowingly and willingly signed away their "lives," many of them their "fortunes," but none of them their "sacred honor."

So concerned, and rightly, was the Continental Congress for the safety of the signers that their names were not revealed for six months after the adoption of the Declaration on July 4, 1776.

When the list was made public, as had been suspected, the British set about to punish as many of the signers as possible. The British succeeded—burning homes, throwing signers and their families into prison, seizing property, and impoverishing many who dared to declare themselves free and independent men.

Through the years since 1776, the Declaration of Independence has been a source of inspiration to people in many nations, for it is a proclamation made on behalf of free men everywhere. Today more than ever, millions of people throughout the world find in the language of the Declaration an expression of their own yearning for freedom and justice, and of their hope for a world in which the words "freedom of choice" will have real meaning. And, today, as on July 4, 1776, these fifty-six who "signed for us" invite each one of us to follow them in subscribing his name to this great document, thus mutually pledging in the cause of Liberty "our lives, our fortunes, and our sacred honor."

In the title of the Declaration the words "United States of America" are used for the first time in any official document. Until then the Colonies were referred to as United Colonies.

If you examine the title carefully you will not find the word "independence," for it is not in the Declaration. "The Declaration of Independence," is a title which has been given by popular use to this immortal document.

"When in the Course of human Events,"

"it becomes necessary for one People"

As John Bull saw it

As the colonists saw it

The argument between the Colonies and Great Britain centered about the definition of the term "one people." The British king insisted that the Colonies were a part of the British Empire and subject to the rule of the king and Parliament. Colonial leaders disagreed; they declared that the colonists themselves were more properly labeled "one people."

The individual Colonies were by no means agreed that they should combine to form a nation with a strong central government such as we have today. There were many colonists who were opposed to centralized authority. These persons favored State governments which were strong and independent.

The question that many colonists asked was this: Did the Declaration of Independence create a *UNITED* States or a United *STATES*?

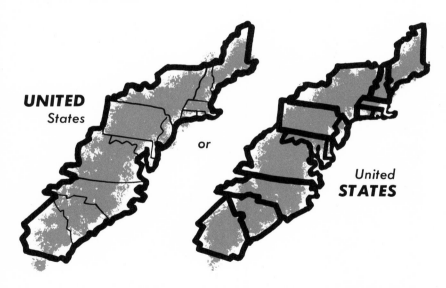

UNITED States or United **STATES**

When the American Revolution began the British considered it a civil war. The colonists were called rebels. However, when the United States declared itself independent, the war became an international war, as far as the rest of the world was concerned. This fact was important to the colonists in seeking loans and other aid from foreign nations.

"to dissolve the Political Bands which have connected them with another"

As John Bull saw it

As the colonists saw it

As John Bull saw it

I'm of age and entitled to be treated as an equal in this family of nations.

As the colonists saw it

The Colonies insisted they were no longer minors in the British family. They demanded to be treated as equals in the family of nations and assume all the rights, burdens, responsibilities, and privileges of international citizenship.

The Colonies insisted that size, wealth, age, and strength were not the basis of international citizenship.

"to which the Laws of Nature"

In this phrase Jefferson is probably referring to what we call today, international law. This is the law, or body of rules, which modern civilized nations regard as binding them in their mutual relationships with each other. This international law did not just happen. It is an outgrowth of universal "right reasoning," present in all countries and with all people. This "right reasoning" or thinking is not dependent upon laws passed by legislatures, parliaments, or other governing bodies. It is inherent in all people who universally accept certain ethical principles. Jefferson said that a logical conclusion of right reasoning was that the United States of America should be given its "separate and equal station" among nations.

"and of Nature's God"

It is apparent that Jefferson, like other philosophers of his time, felt that natural law stems from God's law and could be discovered by man through his powers of reason. The laws of nature are universal in application; so are the divine laws from which the laws of nature come.

Jefferson and his associates felt that it is "right reasoning" to assume that individuals were entitled to consideration as individuals. They also maintained that groups of individuals, such as the citizens of the Colonies, were entitled to equal consideration.

The concern of "Nature's God" for the individual might be suggested by analyzing the word divine. The letter "i" appears twice. One-third of the word is "i".

"entitle them, a decent Respect to the Opinions of Mankind"

"requires that they should declare the causes which impel them to the Separation."

"We hold these Truths to be self-evident,"

The British did not regard the claims of the Colonies as "truths" that would be permanently engraved on the sands of time.

The Colonists maintained their claims were based upon truth; truth that was chiseled on the eternal rocks of the ages.

The rocks, the sand, and the waves are self-evident, and need no proof. The dignity and the importance of the individual, his independence, his right of self-government, are also self-evident and need no proof.

"that all Men are created equal,"

These drops of oil, although differing in size, color, and weight, are equal in their chemical composition and in the eyes of the petroleum engineer. In the refinery, the latent power in each drop is recognized and made usable.

Not necessarily equal physically.

Not necessarily equal mentally.

Not necessarily equal financially.

Not necessarily equal spiritually...

...but equal in the Eyes of the Law.

We are not necessarily equal to others, physically, mentally, spiritually, or financially. But we are equal in our privileges and responsibilities as citizens; and in the Eyes of the Law we all possess the same fundamental rights. The Law is your National Refinery. In its laboratory the powers of each person are made usable.

E QUALITY

You enjoy (E)QUALITY in the eyes of your law. Citizens in some nations do not share the same equality.

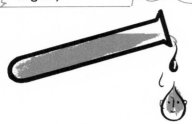

"that they are endowed by their Creator with certain unalienable Rights,"

Each drop of gasoline contains certain properties that are so fundamental that they are innate, or "unalienable," to it. As long as the drop *is* gasoline those properties are a part of it. They are the "life" of the drop; they give it power and flash. This vital spark is not put there by legislation or by any act of government. It cannot be removed by popular vote nor can it be vetoed or repealed. These inborn, "unalienable" rights or properties found in each drop of gasoline were put there by the Creator. Without these properties, the drops cease to be gasoline, and without "certain unalienable rights" people cease to be free.

"that among these are Life, Liberty, and the Pursuit of Happiness—"

In the refining process through which society develops, governments must remember that all people have such rights as "Life, Liberty and the Pursuit of Happiness." These rights do not belong to the government, but to the individual; they are as intimate to you as certain chemical properties are to each drop of crude oil, gasoline, or benzine.

"That to secure these Rights, Governments are instituted among Men,"

These words mean that the purpose of government is to make your rights secure. Jefferson and others maintained that the people do not get their rights from the government; the government gets its powers from the people. The government has no power to give to the people; the people already have the powers. All government can do is to help make your rights secure.

John Adams' statement summed up the case for the people: "You have rights antecedent to all earthly government; rights that cannot be repealed or restrained by human laws; rights derived from the Great Legislator of the Universe." This statement is as true and as important today as it was when Adams made it.

As John Bull saw it

GOVERNmenT

As the colonists saw it

governMENt

The difference in emphasis in these words illustrated the differing philosophies of government held by the British monarch and the American patriots.

Sign of Tyranny

Sign of Liberty

For hundreds of years governments had insisted that people were responsible *TO* government; the colonists insisted the people were responsible *FOR* government.

The only "just powers" your government has are powers which come directly from the people. As long as the people keep their hands on the power pump, the machines of your government will be kept under control. Whenever the people get careless or surrender their powers, tyranny is not far away.

The colonists knew tyranny from bitter experience.

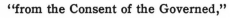

"from the Consent of the Governed,"

By revolution, bloodshed, and sacrifice man has gained his freedom from tyrants. The colonists maintained that the rights of the people were the only divine rights. They intended to set up a government upon that principle.

Their slogan was not, "the consent of the govern*ing*;" but, "the consent of the govern*ed*."

"that whenever any Form of Government becomes destructive of these Ends, it is the Right of the People to alter or to abolish it, and to institute new Government,"

INTERNATIONAL GOVERNMENTAL MACHINES

SALESROOM

I might put a new motor in or I might have the machinery of government overhauled.

I don't recommend it Sam. Get a new model that will last you for generations.

The British monarch was shocked by the colonists' declaration that they could change their type of government when and if they chose. But the colonists insisted that those who were governing were not so important as those being governed. They felt that a governmental official had no particular right to his office; he held it only as long as the people wished.

Therefore, not only could the office holder be removed, but the office itself could be abolished and even the government under which the office was set up.

This could happen if the people so desired.

"laying its Foundation on such Principles, and organizing its Powers in such Form, as to them shall seem most likely to effect their Safety and Happiness."

DIGNITY OF THE INDIVIDUAL

"Prudence, indeed, will dictate that Governments long established should not be changed for light and transient Causes;"

The authors of the Declaration recognized the necessity of a stable government not subject to change by short-sighted or selfish politicians.

"and accordingly all Experience hath shewn, that Mankind are more disposed to suffer, while Evils are sufferable, than to right themselves by abolishing the Forms to which they are accustomed."

People hesitate to make basic and fundamental change—especially in their government. They will suffer much abuse before they finally act.

"But when a long Train of Abuses and Usurpations, pursuing invariably the same Object, evinces a Design to reduce them under absolute Despotism,"

"it is their Right, it is their Duty, to throw off such Government, and to provide new Guards for their future Security."

40

"The History of the present King of Great Britain is a History of repeated Injuries and Usurpations, all having in direct Object the Establishment of an absolute Tyranny over these States."

Many colonists would have been willing to make peace with the king and Parliament if the British had been willing to repeal offensive legislation.

"To prove this, let Facts be submitted to a candid World."

To a fair and impartial world

Specific Charges Against King George

In some instances the king had vetoed laws passed by colonial legislatures. On other occasions he had refused to permit the British Parliament to pass much needed legislation, requested by the colonists.

HAD THESE EVENTS HAPPENED TODAY:

You would understand how the colonists felt if, in spite of the expressed wishes of the people, the President of the United States were able to prevent the passage of sorely needed laws.

That this might not happen to YOU

Article 1, Section 7, Clause 2, of the Constitution provides a means by which the veto of the President can be overridden. It also provides that if the President does not return a bill with his signature or his veto within ten days the bill becomes a law without the signature of the President.

"He has forbidden his Governors to pass Laws of immediate and pressing Importance, unless suspended in their Operation till his Assent should be obtained; and when so suspended, he has utterly neglected to attend to them."

Permit no laws to be passed in your states which I, the President, have not personally approved in advance. Perhaps I will approve them and perhaps I will not.

Suppose that a situation developed in this country which made it possible for the President to require his personal approval of all legislation in advance of its passage. Then suppose that, without giving any reason, he refused to approve laws that had the support of a great majority of people. You would be faced with much the same situation the colonists were, and you would understand why they protested strongly against this arrangement.

That this might not happen to YOU

Article 1, Section 7, Clause 2, of your Constitution provides a method by which the veto of the President can be overridden.

Article 1, Section 2, Clause 5, and Article 1, Section 3, Clause 6, provide for the impeachment of the President, your Chief Executive.

"He has refused to pass other Laws for the Accommodation of large Districts of People, unless those People would relinquish the Right of Representation in the Legislature, a Right inestimable to them, and formidable to Tyrants only."

To the colonists, being denied representation in the legislature in return for more local units of government made about as much sense as riding backwards on a horse.

Travel in colonial America was a serious problem; roads were few and usable only in good weather. When seats of government were inconveniently located, a real hardship was created for people who needed to record deeds, obtain licenses, transfer titles to land, or obtain other services from the government. People in many Colonies began to demand the establishment of more local seats of government within easy traveling distance.

Most colonial governments consisted of three bodies: a governor, a council, and an assembly. In most cases the governor and council were appointed by the king or the proprietor; the assembly was usually popularly elected and was composed of representatives from the towns, villages, and counties. As the number of governmental units grew, so did

the size of the assembly. The king, concerned at the growing size and importance of the assemblies, decreed that new towns and villages could be created but that they could not be given

representation in the assemblies. The colonists were told
that they could have more local seats of government, but *not*
"unless those people would relinquish the right of Representation in the Legislature . . ."

From the colonists' point of view, being denied representation in the legislature was comparable to being given a service
station with neither gas nor oil.

This illustrates in modern terms how the colonists saw matters in 1776.

That this might not happen to YOU

In Article 1, Section 2, Clause 3, of your Constitution provision is made for a population census every ten years. This census is used as a basis for representation in the House of Representatives, and for many other purposes.

49

These wrongs will not happen again if YOU

(a) Elect to office honest, efficient, intelligent, freedom-loving officials.

(b) Keep your congressmen and state legislators informed of your opinions.

(c) Let the President of the United States and the governor of your State know about the laws you wish them to sign or veto.

(d) Urge the impeachment of the President or your governor if either violates his oath of office.

(e) Remember yourself, and remind your officials, that yours is a government of LAWS, not of men.

(f) Are LOYAL to the spirit and the letter of:
(1) The Constitution of the United States
(2) The constitution of your State.

(g) Urge your friends and associates to be LOYAL.

(h) Vote intelligently at every election and on every candidate and issue.

(i) Actively support your worthy officials.

(j) Co-operate with the U.S. Census Bureau when the census is taken each ten years.

(k) Interest yourself and your neighbors in congressional reapportionment, and let your State legislature know of your interest.

"He has called together Legislative Bodies at Places unusual, uncomfortable, and distant from the Depository of their public Records, for the sole Purpose of fatiguing them into Compliance with his Measures."

The colonists bitterly protested the actions of certain royal governors who convened sessions of the Assembly in places that were not easy to reach, and that were far from their homes and their records. These places were deliberately chosen, the people said, to make it as difficult as possible for the colonists to attend, in the hope that they would grow discouraged and give in to the demands of the king.

If the President were to call a session of Congress to meet aboard ship, or if the governor of your State ordered a special session of the legislature to meet in an isolated or out-of-the-way spot, this would be comparable to the situation faced by the colonists.

That this might not happen to YOU

Article 1, Section 8, Clause 17, of your Constitution authorizes Congress to establish a fixed location for the seat of the federal government (Washington, D. C.). State constitutions also make provision for the location of State capitals and county seats.

"He has dissolved Representative Houses repeatedly, for opposing with manly Firmness his Invasions on the Rights of the People."

The Royal Governor told you not to play legislature without his permission.

On several occasions the British Government had "dissolved Representative Houses" for insisting on their rights. The Virginia House of Burgesses had been dissolved three times; but each time the representatives met in a tavern in Williamsburg and finished their business. In Massachusetts, South Carolina, and Georgia, legislatures had also been dissolved.

A comparable situation today would be created if the governor of a State used the State militia (National Guard) to "dissolve" or adjourn the legislature without legal authority.

That this might not happen to YOU

The federal Constitution and the constitutions of each of the fifty States all provide specific times and places for legislative meetings.

"He has refused for a long Time, after such Dissolutions, to cause others to be elected; whereby the Legislative Powers, incapable of Annihilation, have returned to the People at large for their exercise; the State remaining in the meantime exposed to all the Dangers of invasion from without, and Convulsions within."

In several of the Colonies such as North Carolina, Massachusetts, and Virginia, legislative bodies met in spite of the fact that by royal decree the assemblies had been dissolved. Just as each drop of gasoline contains power of its own, apart from the rest of the tank, so each citizen possesses rights which are his regardless of any action or inaction of government. When the government (the engine) fails to function, the people (the drops of gasoline) may apply their power to another machine.

When government fails to carry out its responsibilities, the people have a right to act on their own behalf. There is no power vacuum when a government fails. The people simply take back the authority which they had voluntarily delegated to their government in the first place. They must do this in order to protect themselves. ". . . the State remaining in the meantime exposed to all the Dangers of invasion from without, and Convulsions within."

If this tyrant will not let us meet in the Capital Building we'll meet somewhere else. The powers belong to the people, not him.

Imagine the popular outcry that would result if a President or governor tried to prevent the meeting of legislative bodies today, and laws necessary to your security went unconsidered. The people would demand that their legislatures be assembled and that business as usual be resumed. Inasmuch as the basic source of authority is in YOU, it is up to YOU to make certain that no similar condition ever develops again in YOUR country.

That this might not happen to YOU

Article 1, Section 2, Clause 1; Article 1, Section 3, Clause 1; Article 1, Section 4, Clause 1; and the 17th amendment of your Constitution provide for the popular election of representatives and senators.

Amendment 1 declares that "Congress shall make no law respecting . . . the right of the people peaceably to assemble, and to petition the government for a redress of grievances."

"He has endeavoured to prevent the Population of these States; for that purpose obstructing the Laws for Naturalization of Foreigners; refusing to pass others to encourage their Migrations hither, and raising the Conditions of new Appropriations of Lands."

In 1763 the king issued a royal proclamation which forbade the colonists to settle in the region west of the Alleghenies, thereby ". . . raising the conditions of new Appropriations of Lands." Probably the king and Parliament intended this to be a temporary measure, but the colonists interpreted it as a deliberate attempt to block the westward movement in order to benefit English land speculators and fur traders.

Suppose the President announced, "No one may move west of the Ohio or Mississippi rivers"; and, in order to enforce his edict, restricted immigration to the United States. You would then understand how the colonists felt when the king interfered with their plans for settling the West.

That this might not happen to YOU

Article 1, Section 8, Clause 4, of your Constitution provides for a "... uniform rule of naturalization ..."

Article 1, Section 10, Clause 2, provides that States may not, without the consent of Congress, interfere with the trade of other States.

Article 4, Section 2, Clause 1, provides that "citizens of each State shall be entitled to all privileges and immunities of citizens in the several States."

These wrongs will not happen again if YOU

(a) Elect to office candidates who will insist upon seeing that your rights are protected.

(b) Keep a close check on your congressmen and State legislators to see that they are present when Congress and your legislature assemble and that your representatives attend to your business carefully.

(c) Make it your business to meet, to talk with, to listen to, or to become acquainted with the candidates for public office. Then vote for those who stand for the principles which you approve.

(d) Become acquainted with the naturalization laws of the United States and how they function.

(e) Let Congress know how you feel if the laws are not what you think they should be.

(f) Insist that other States do not deny citizens of your State the "privileges and immunities of citizens in the several States."

(g) Remember yourself, and remind your officials, that yours is a goverment of LAWS, not of men.

(h) Are LOYAL to the spirit and the letter of:
    (1) The Constitution of the United States
    · (2) The constitution of your State.

(i) Urge your friends and associates to be LOYAL.

(j) Vote intelligently at every election and on every candidate and issue.

(k) Actively support your worthy officials.

"He has obstructed the Administration of Justice, by refusing his Assent to Laws for establishing Judiciary Powers."

In North Carolina there had been a bitter argument between the colonial legislature and the royal governor. As a result, the laws which created the courts were not re-enacted when they expired. This left North Carolina without courts for more than a year. Such a situation became intolerable. South Carolina, Pennsylvania, and Virginia also had difficulties with the British regarding courts of law.

63

If suddenly one morning a sign over your courthouse read, "Closed by Order of the President" you would know how the colonists felt. Try to imagine the chaos that would result. Your police and fire departments would not function; no criminals would be apprehended; no real estate could be recorded and in general, no public business conducted. What would you do?

That this might not happen to YOU.

Article 3, Section 1, of your Constitution provides for the establishment of a system of courts and describes the "... judicial power of the United States ..."

Article 3, Section 2, Clause 1, outlines the scope of the federal courts. State constitutions make provisions for State courts.

> "He has made Judges dependent on his Will alone, for the Tenure of their Offices, and the Amount and Payment of their Salaries."

Several Colonies had serious quarrels over the status of their judges. How long should judges serve? Who should pay their salaries? To whom should they answer? To the Crown? To the people of the Colonies? These were the burning legal questions of the hour. Most colonists felt that the judges should be completely independent of British control and accountable only to the colonists themselves. Others, especially the pro-British, felt that the judges were a part of the British legal system and should be appointed by and responsible to the Crown. The men who signed the Declaration of Independence made it clear that they felt the judges were too dependent on the king.

HAD THESE EVENTS HAPPENED TODAY:

PRESIDENT CONTROLS JUDGES

With a bold stroke unauthorized by Congress, the President yesterday announced that all judges will be dependent on his will alone, for the tenure of their offices, and the amount and payment of their salaries.

Can you imagine the storm of protest that would follow an announcement like the one above? This arrangement could enable the party in power to control the courts of law. Politicians could then bring pressure on judges to punish the enemies of their party and others who might attempt to interfere with their plans or goals. You would not like this. Neither did the signers of the Declaration of Independence. We insist that judges be free from interference from anyone; that their pay be independent of any President, governor, or other individual. A free judiciary is one of the most important foundations of our democracy.

That this might not happen to YOU

Article 3, Section 1, of your Constitution provides that federal judges ". . . shall hold their offices during good behavior . . ." It also provides that their salary ". . . shall not be diminished during their continuance in office."

"He has erected a Multitude of new Offices, and sent hither Swarms of Officers to harrass our People, and eat out their Substance."

As John Bull saw it

In order for the British to enforce laws against smuggling and certain laws dealing with trade between the Colonies and other countries, customs officers were appointed and special courts were established. The British contended these courts would assist the colonists in getting quick justice and at the same time serve the interests of the Crown.

As the colonists saw it

The colonists protested the creation of these new offices, which they regarded as potential instruments of tyranny. They were especially resentful because they were expected to furnish the funds to sustain the unwanted agencies.

How would you react if the governor of your State, without the consent of the legislature, appointed "Swarms of Officers to harass" you, and then raised your taxes to pay their salaries? Today you have a voice in the appointment of "Officers" through your legislature. If you do not approve of what your officials do, you can remove them at the next election. The colonists did not enjoy this privilege.

That this might not happen to YOU

Article 1, Section 9, Clause 7, of your Constitution provides that "No money shall be drawn from the treasury, but in consequence of appropriations made by law . . ." All State constitutions have similar provisions.

"He has kept among us, in Times of Peace, Standing Armies, without the consent of our Legislatures."

The British monarch believed he was completely within his rights in stationing troops in the American Colonies, in time of peace as well as in time of war. But since the days of James II, the British people had objected to standing armies which were not authorized by Parliament and such armies were forbidden by the English Bill of Rights. The colonists were merely echoing this objection when they protested the establishment of peace-time armies that did not have the approval of colonial legislatures.

Our Constitution prevents the maintaining of large standing armies unless Congress approves. In fact, so concerned were the colonists over the matter of "standing Armies" that a provision was made in the Constitution that "no appropriation of money to that use shall be for a longer term than two years." Thus you are protected from a repetition of what happened to the colonists.

That this might not happen to YOU

Article 1, Section 8, Clause 12, of your Constitution provides that ". . . no appropriation of money [to support the armies] . . . shall be for a longer term than two years."

Also, Article 1, Section 10, Clause 3, provides that "No State shall, without the consent of Congress, . . . keep troops or ships of war in time of peace . . ."

While he was commander-in-chief of the British troops in America, General Gage was made governor of Massachusetts. This appointment angered many of the colonists as it appeared to them to "render the Military independent of and superior to the Civil Power," which in fact it did.

General Gage had previously claimed military superiority to civil authority in other Colonies in which he had been stationed.

71

As chairman of the Joint Chiefs of Staff of the Armed Forces of the United States, I do hereby declare that from this moment the Armed Forces of this nation are independent and superior to all civil authority. We shall levy our own taxes.

Were this to happen today we would recognize it as a grave threat to our Liberty, just as the colonists did.

That this might not happen to YOU

Article 1, Section 8, Clause 12, of your Constitution limits all military appropriations to a two-year period.

Article 1, Section 10, Clause 3, provides that no troops or ships of war shall be kept in time of peace without the consent of Congress.

Article 2, Section 2, Clause 1, establishes the President as commander-in-chief of the armed forces. The President, a civilian elected by the people, thus "outranks" all officers of the Army, Navy, and Air Force.

72

These wrongs will not happen again if YOU

(a) Urge the impeachment of the President if he violates his oath of office to uphold the Constitution of the United States.

(b) Urge your Congress or legislature to withhold appropriations from the military if it acts unconstitutionally.

(c) Respect the decisions of the courts, and encourage others to do so.

(d) Insist that your State and federal judiciary be kept free from political and other influences that would interfere with judges rendering fair and honest decisions.

(e) Insist that the appointment and election of judges be done in such a way that only the best candidates will be chosen.

(f) Remember yourself, and remind your officials, that yours is a government of LAWS, not of men.

(g) Are LOYAL to the spirit and the letter of:
   (1) The Constitution of the United States
   (2) The constitution of your State.

(h) Urge your friends and associates to be LOYAL.

(i) Vote intelligently at every election and on every candidate and issue.

(j) Actively support your worthy officials.

(k) As a citizen appeal to the courts in your community to require any elected or appointed public official or body:
   (1) To carry out the duties of his or their office
   (2) To stop doing any unauthorized or illegal act.

"He has combined with others to subject us to a Jurisdiction foreign to our Constitution, and unacknowledged by our Laws; giving his Assent to their Acts of pretended Legislation :"

As John Bull saw it

As the colonists saw it

This clause in the Declaration touches one of the basic points at issue in the dispute between Britain and the Colonies: the question of legislative authority. Parliament declared that it had the right to ". . . make laws and statutes . . . to bind the Colonies in all cases whatsoever." Although colonial leaders were not in agreement as to the exact extent of Parliament's powers, they all denied that it possessed any such sweeping authority. Many colonists conceded to Parliament the right to regulate trade; but not the right to tax the Colonies. The more enthusiastic patriots maintained that the Colonies were politically self-sufficient and should be free to govern themselves. They observed that the British people looked to their Parliament for protection against tyranny, yet seemed to accept the idea that Parliament could oppress the colonists if necessary to attain British ends.

Jefferson and his associates declared that the colonial legislatures were their "parliaments," and to these legislatures they would look for protection and aid. "Our Constitution" according to Jefferson was not based on the actions of the British Parliament in London, but was established by the representative bodies elected by the people of the Colonies.

The authors of the Declaration of Independence accused the king of "combining with others" (i.e. the members of Parliament) to make laws that were not in the best interests of the colonists and, indeed, were foreign to their "Constitution."

75

Suppose that the President, being commander-in-chief of the armed forces, sent an army to California and by force, or other equally offensive means, "dissolved" the California legislature and refused to permit it to meet.

But the Army has forbidden the California legislature to meet. The New York legislature is in charge of our affairs.

What does New York know about California's affairs.

Suppose that the President then gave the governor of New York and the New York legislature jurisdiction over the affairs of California.

Suppose further that the New York legislature passed certain laws opposed by Californians and refused to pass others advocated by them.

And while your "Supposer" is working, suppose there were no radio, no television, no telegraph, no airplanes, no trains, no steamships, and no autos, and that the only means of receiving and transmitting messages between New York and California were overland by covered wagon or by a long sea voyage around the tip of South America.

If you will lump all these "supposes" together, you will appreciate what Jefferson meant when he protested against ". . . a jurisdiction foreign to our Constitution, and unacknowledged by our Laws . . ."

That this might not happen to YOU

Amendments 9 and 10, of your Constitution place the powers of government unmistakably in the hands of the people.

Amendment 14, Section 1, provides "No State shall make or enforce any law which shall abridge the privileges or immunities of citizens of the United States . . ."

77

LATEST INSULT

The King and Parliament demand

1. That we furnish quarters for British troops whenever, wherever those troops are stationed.

2. That we pay for this quartering, and for certain supplies.

Under the Quartering Act of 1765, Parliament attempted to force the colonists to provide living quarters for British troops. Another act in 1774 required colonists to furnish shelter to troops even when military barracks were available in the vicinity, if the British considered the barracks inconveniently located.

Parliament ordered the colonial legislatures to reimburse individual colonists whose property and/or supplies were used to support the British Army. But the situation proved intolerable to the colonists. They had no way of knowing where, when, or how many troops would be stationed in certain areas. And they bitterly resented the intrusions on their privacy.

HAD THESE EVENTS HAPPENED TODAY:

Such a situation, were it reenacted today, would be as objectionable to us as it was to the colonists. They included the Quartering Act of 1774 among the so-called "Intolerable Acts."

That this might not happen to YOU

Amendment 3 of your Constitution prohibits quartering of troops in time of peace in private homes without the consent of the owner, ". . . nor in time of war, but in a manner to be prescribed by law."

79

"For protecting them, by a mock Trial, from Punishment for any Murders which they should commit on the Inhabitants of these States :"

After the Boston Massacre, Parliament passed a law which stated that prosecution of British officials for murder or other high offense need not be carried out in the locality where the offense was committed. According to this law, British soldiers accused of murder might be tried in another Colony or in Britain itself. Under the circumstances colonists regarded such a trial as "a mock Trial." They declared that this ruling made it possible for agents of the British government to escape punishment for their crimes.

What right has a militia man from the State of Delaware to shoot one of our Texans who was resisting an illegal interference.

The imaginary incident depicted above shows why the colonists objected to the British policy, and why the authors of the Declaration of Independence included the "mock Trial" passage. For in addition to protecting the Delaware militia-man from arrest and punishment, the British law would have provided that any Texan who participated in the incident, or witnessed it, could be taken to Delaware for trial. Although such witnesses would be paid a fee to cover their expenses, the amount of the fee would be determined arbitrarily by the governor of Delaware.

That this might not happen to YOU

Article 3, Section 2, Clause 3, of your Constitution provides that all criminal trials shall be by jury, and ". . . shall be held in the State where the said crimes shall have been committed."

Amendment 6 provides that ". . . the accused shall enjoy the right to a speedy and public trial, by an impartial jury of the State and district wherein the crime shall have been committed . . ."

The British had enacted many trade regulations which made it virtually impossible for the Colonies to do business with any nation other than Britain. In addition to attempting to establish a monopoly on colonial trade, Britain also imposed taxes and numerous restrictions upon the merchants who were engaged in buying and selling abroad. These interferences were annoying to the colonists and caused financial hardship to many of them.

You may trade only with our country, and what is more we are going to close Boston, New York, and San Francisco harbors to all trade. We may also close others.

We will see about that.

That this might not happen to YOU

Article 1, Section 8, Clause 3, of your Constitution gives Congress power to regulate not only our country's foreign trade, but also trade between the States themselves. Thus Congress could take any action necessary to prevent unwarranted interference with American commerce.

Nothing angered the colonists more than the many taxes imposed on them by Parliament without the consent of colonial legislatures. Among such acts were the Stamp Act of 1765 and the Townshend Acts passed two years later.

The colonists maintained that since they were not represented in the British Parliament, they could not legally be taxed by it. The cry of, "Taxation without representation is tyranny" was echoed throughout the Colonies.

84

Suppose the President or the governor of your State established a special "Revenue Raising Committee" which proceeded to levy taxes on you and your community without consulting you or obtaining your approval. From the viewpoint of the colonists, this situation would be very similar to the one they faced. How would you react?

That this might not happen to YOU

Article 1, Section 7, Clause 1, of your Constitution provides "All bills for raising revenue shall originate in the House of Representatives . . ."

Article 1, Section 8, Clause 1, and Amendment 16 give Congress ". . . power to lay and collect taxes . . ."

All State constitutions have similar provisions guaranteeing popular control of tax-raising authority.

Admiralty Courts tried all cases dealing with offenses committed on the high seas, or involving collection of customs duties or other matters pertaining to trade. British law provided special types of trials for persons charged with such violations. These trials were conducted in British courts, by judges appointed by the Crown, and without juries.

CONSTITUTION OF THE UNITED STATES OF AMERICA
Article 3, Section 2, Clause 3.
"The trial of all crimes . . . shall be by jury."

Except all cases that involve custom duties, manufacturing taxs, trade affairs and United States Government affairs

Suppose that without your consent federal officials declared that all crimes involving imports and exports, manufacturing, trade, and government revenues were to be tried without juries. Then add to that the hazard of being tried in courts whose judges received their salaries and held their jobs at the pleasure of the high officials bringing the charges.

This situation would be comparable to the one which the colonists faced.

That this might not happen to YOU

Article 3, Section 2, Clause 3, and Amendments 5 and 6 of your Constitution guarantee trial by jury.

State constitutions also make provisions for jury trial.

> "For transporting us beyond Seas to be tried for pretended Offences:"

SCENE OF ALLEGED CRIME.

COULD BE TRIED IN REMOTE PLACES

Atlantic Ocean

Parliament had passed an act stating that Americans could be taken to England for trial or to give testimony as witnesses. The king had also decreed that cases having to do with customs duties and certain other taxes could be tried in Admiralty Courts anywhere in the British realm, without jury trials. Thus American colonists could be taken to England or anywhere else in the British Empire, and be made to stand trial before unfriendly judges. Under this procedure, the accused could be tried in a place thousands of miles distant from the witnesses and records necessary to his defense.

That this might not happen to YOU

Article 3, Section 2, Clause 3, and Amendment 6 of your Constitution provide that criminal trials be held within the State or district in which the alleged crime was committed.

"For abolishing the free System of English Laws in a neighbouring Province, establishing therein an arbitrary Government, and enlarging its Boundaries so as to render it at once an Example and fit Instrument for introducing the same absolute Rule into these Colonies:"

The Quebec Act, passed on June 22, 1774, extended the boundaries of Quebec to include a large portion of the territory between the Ohio and the Mississippi Rivers. In this territory French *civil* law was established, although in criminal matters the English code remained in effect. The government was vested in a council and a governor both appointed by the Crown. There was no representative assembly until many years later.

This expansion of Quebec halted the westward migration of the colonists, and at the same time restricted the expansion of the British system of common law under which the Colonies functioned. This meant that the institutions of free government to which the colonists had grown accustomed would not be allowed to develop in the West.

HAD THESE EVENTS HAPPENED TODAY:

If the Quebec Act were re-enacted today the territory now occupied by Wisconsin, Michigan, Illinois, Ohio, and Indiana would be annexed to Quebec. A quick look at the map would show that there could be no westward expansion from New York, Connecticut, Massachusetts, and Virginia, all of which claimed territory in this great northwestern area. Furthermore:

(1) Our common law and many of the freedoms we enjoy under it would be replaced by French civil law.

(2) The territory would be governed by an appointed governor and legislative council, rather than one elected by popular vote of the people.

These conditions would be as confusing and objectionable to us now as they were to the colonists then.

That this might not happen to YOU

Article 4, Section 3, Clause 1, of your Constitution places control of the creation and admission of new States to the Union in the hands of Congress, which is elected by the people and is accountable to them.

> "For taking away our Charters, abolishing our most valuable Laws, and altering fundamentally the Forms of our Governments:"

State House
Boston, Mass.

This charge resulted from the Massachusetts Government Act, which was one of the "Intolerable Acts" passed by Parliament following the Boston Tea Party in 1773. This act drastically altered the Charter of Massachusetts. It provided that:

(1) The upper house of the Massachusetts legislature, the Council, was to be appointed by the royal governor. (It had been traditionally elected by the people.)

(2) The justice of the peace, the sheriff, and certain other local officials were also to become royal appointees.

(3) Juries were to be appointed by the sheriff, rather than elected by the people.

In addition to these changes the royal governor moved the meeting place of the Massachusetts assembly from Boston to Cambridge. He also attempted to make the judges of Massachusetts dependent on the British government, rather than on the assembly, for their salaries. To the colonists these actions were equivalent to "taking away our Charter."

We can understand the feelings of the colonists when we consider how the king's acts would affect us today. Suppose we awoke one morning to learn that the governor had declared his intention to:

(1) Appoint all the members of the upper house of the legislature.

(2) Appoint the sheriffs, whom he would then empower to select all jurymen.

(3) Be personally responsible for the payment of salaries to all judges, thus making them responsible to him, not to the people.

(4) Move the State Capitol to another location away from the records and data needed by members of the legislature.

You would be outraged by these actions; so were the colonists. If the governor could set aside the State constitution at will, what would become of our liberties?

That this might not happen to YOU

Article 5 of your Constitution establishes clearly defined methods by which the constitutional foundation of the government may be altered. All State constitutions have similar provisions.

> "For suspending our own Legislatures, and declaring themselves invested with Power to legislate for us in all Cases whatsoever."

Because the New York legislature had not met all of the conditions imposed by Parliament for the support of British troops, it was suspended in 1767. (Later, however, the legislature voted the funds necessary to comply with Parliament's demands and it was again permitted to meet).

In 1766, after having repealed the detested Stamp Act, Parliament defiantly passed a Declaratory Act. In this measure Parliament asserted that it had the right to make laws for ". . . the colonies and people of America, subjects of the crown of Great Britain, in all cases whatsoever." This act seemed to threaten an end to self-government in the Colonies; for, of what value was local government if Parliament could pass any acts it desired?

Suppose the federal government established a military post in your State, declaring that it must be supported solely by local taxes; and, until your State agreed to this arrangement, there would be no meetings of your legislature. Then suppose Congress declared itself invested with power to legislate for you in "all cases whatsoever." (Remember that *this* Congress would be composed of members who were not chosen by the people, and who were not even residents of your country.) You would then be in a position very much like that of the American colonists in 1776.

That this might not happen to YOU

Article 1, Section 4, Clause 2, and Amendment 20 of your Constitution provide for an annual meeting of the Congress.

Amendments 9 and 10 establish the fact that the powers of government belong to the people.

These wrongs will not happen again if YOU

(a) Do not permit any agency of government to assume powers that belong to YOU.

(b) Do not pass to government *responsibilities* which YOU should assume.

(c) Discourage your legislature from making laws which are unfair to citizens of other States.

(d) Refuse to permit the invasion of your privacy or of your property without proper consent.

(e) Keep in touch with your congressmen and your State legislators to let them know that you have an active interest in such matters as taxation and trade.

(f) Lend your support to accepted organizations which carefully observe and report on the actions of public agencies.

(g) Permit no tampering with your courts or juries.

(h) Encourage the free press, radio, and television to act as guardians of the liberties of the people.

(i) Remember yourself, and remind your officials that yours is a government of LAWS, not of men.

(j) Are LOYAL to the spirit and the letter of:
    (1) The Constitution of the United States
    (2) The constitution of your State.

(k) Urge your friends and associates to be LOYAL.

(l) Vote intelligently at every election and on every candidate and issue.

(m) Actively support your worthy officials.

(n) As a citizen appeal to the courts in your community to require any elected or appointed public official or body:
    (1) To carry out the duties of his or their office
    (2) To stop doing any unauthorized or illegal act.

"He has abdicated Government here, by declaring us out of his Protection and waging War against us."

Following the fighting at Lexington, Concord, and Bunker Hill in the spring of 1775, the governors of New York, Virginia, North Carolina, and South Carolina took refuge in various places, leaving those Colonies without executive leadership. Then in August, 1775, the king issued a royal proclamation declaring the Colonies to be in a state of rebellion. The colonists felt that the king had in effect, "abdicated Government" and declared them "Out of his Protection."

You can imagine the confusion that would exist in your State if the governor left indefinitely and there were no lieutenant-governor to act in his behalf.

That this might not happen to YOU

Article 2, Section 1, Clause 6, of your Constitution provides that "In case of the removal of the President from office, or of his death, resignation, or inability to discharge the powers and duties of the said office . . ." the Vice-President assumes the duties of the President.

Article 1, Section 2, Clause 5; and Article 1, Section 3, Clause 6, provide for the impeachment of the President.

All State constitutions have similar provisions relating to the governors.

"He has plundered our Seas, ravaged our Coasts, burnt our Towns, and destroyed the Lives of our People."

Here Jefferson refers to the virtual state of war that existed between the Colonies and the mother country early in 1776. British ships had blockaded the coast and preyed on colonial shipping. During the hostilities several colonial towns—Norfolk, Virginia; Charlestown, Massachusetts (now part of Boston); Charleston, South Carolina; and Falmouth (Portland), Maine—had been burned and a number of inhabitants killed.

100

As commander-in-chief of the armed forces the President has far greater military force at his command today than the king of England possessed in 1776. That he would ever consider using it to punish or coerce a State is, of course, most unlikely. None the less there are important constitutional safeguards against misuse of executive power.

That this might not happen to YOU

Article 1, Section 2, Clause 5, and Article 1, Section 3, Clause 6, of your Constitution, provide for the impeachment of the President.

Amendment 2 provides for the maintenance of State militia.

Amendment 4 provides against unwarranted searches and seizures.

101

"He is, at this Time, transporting large Armies of foreign Mercenaries to compleat the Works of Death, Desolation, and Tyranny, already begun with circumstances of Cruelty and Perfidy, scarcely paralleled in the most barbarous Ages, and totally unworthy the Head of a civilized Nation."

Unable to get enough men to police the Colonies, King George III resorted to hiring thousands of mercenary soldiers from Germany. They were called Hessians because most of them came from Hesse, a province of Germany. Few actions of the king were more bitterly denounced by the colonists than the employment of foreign troops.

If our President assumed unconstitutional powers and then hired foreign troops to prevent you from defending your rights, you would understand how the colonists felt.

That this might not happen to YOU

Article 1, Section 2, Clause 5, and Article 1, Section 3, Clause 6, of your Constitution provide for the impeachment of the President.

Article 1, Section 8, Clause 12, limits military appropriations to a term of two years.

"He has constrained our fellow Citizens taken Captive on the high Seas to bear Arms against their Country, to become the Executioners of their Friends and Brethren, or to fall themselves by their Hands."

You are stealing my cargo and forcing my seamen to fight their own brothers and fathers. If they desert you will treat them as traitors to the British Navy which they never joined.

In December of 1775, Parliament adopted a measure which proved so oppressive that it alienated many colonists who had remained, up to that time, loyal to the king and opposed to the idea of independence. By the terms of the new law any vessel engaged in trade with the Colonies could be seized, its cargo confiscated, and its officers and crew "impressed" into the British Navy. This drastic measure forced some colonists to fight against their own countrymen.

"He has excited domestic Insurrections amongst us, and has endeavoured to bring on the Inhabitants of our Frontiers, the merciless Indian Savages, whose known Rule of Warfare, is an undistinguished Destruction, of all Ages, Sexes, and Conditions."

In an effort to crush uprisings among the colonists, British agents attempted to incite "domestic insurrection" among the slaves in the Colonies, and to provoke Indian warfare on the frontier. In Virginia and both of the Carolinas, representatives of the Crown were known to be involved in plots to free the slaves and enlist their aid, and that of the Indians, to fight the colonists.

"LET ALL AMERICANS

STAND GUARD..."

During a dark hour of the War for Independence, General George Washington sent word to his high command: "Let only Americans stand guard tonight."

Today few of us are called on to suffer cold, hunger and hardships for our country; nor are we asked to risk "our lives, our fortunes, and our sacred honor."

Seldom are we required to make personal sacrifices to protect our freedom, as were the colonists to gain theirs.

Today our nation is in grave danger of losing its liberties—*our* liberties. Freedom always is in danger. As long as free men are on earth, tyrants cannot rest. We believe with the Founding Fathers, that men "... are endowed by their Creator with certain unalienable Rights, that among these are Life, Liberty, and the pursuit of Happiness." Dictators insist on the exact opposite; namely, that the people have only those rights which the *state* chooses to give them.

When things were going badly for the colonial cause Thomas Paine wrote: "Tyranny . . . is not easily conquered. What we obtain too cheap, we esteem too lightly . . . It would be strange indeed if so celestial an article as freedom should not be highly rated."

Each American, whatever his ancestry, creed or philosophy, must stand guard tonight, tomorrow, and in the future, if the flame of freedom is to continue to burn.

The United States of America is not the first republic in history. May it not be the last! Freedom has been won and lost in other countries. It is doubtful that we in our country would ever regain our right of choice were we to lose it. Modern weapons, available to tyrants, are too powerful for ordinary citizens to combat.

A prominent official of a government where the dignity and worth of the individual are *not* recognized said: "America will someday adopt our philosophy of life . . . We can wait. Time and history are on our side."

Whether this ominous prophecy comes true depends largely on two factors:

(1) Our being conquered by another power
(2) Our voluntarily abandoning American ideals and institutions—our very way of life.

Ours is a political and economic system that has brought more happiness to more people on this earth than any other system in history. Who will decide what type of government we shall live under—tomorrow and in the near and distant future? The decision will be made by:

(1) Those who go regularly to the polls
(2) Those who stay away from the polls.

Government is everybody's business:
"Let only Americans stand guard tonight!"

> "In every stage of these Oppressions we have Petitioned for Redress in the most humble Terms: Our repeated Petitions have been answered only by repeated Injury."

The colonists had petitioned in a respectful, dignified, yet firm way. "In every stage of these Oppressions" the colonists had voiced their objections—to the royal governors, to Parliament directly, and to King George III personally.

Many members of Parliament urged a reasonable and fair attitude toward the Colonies. Notable speeches of conciliation were made, some of which are still read as good literature in the field of pre-Revolutionary War days. The king ignored the good advice given him, and with the co-operation of Parliament, continued his repressive policies toward the American Colonies.

If petitions which you sent to Congress, the President, and your State government officials were ignored, torn up, and treated with scorn, and you had no way of removing such arrogant officials from office, you would readily appreciate the anger and frustration felt by the colonists.

That this might not happen to YOU

Amendment 1 to your Constitution reads "Congress shall make no law respecting . . . the right of the people . . . to petition the government . . ." All State constitutions contain a similar provision which applies to State legislatures.

The President of the United States and the governor of every State are answerable to the people on election day, and can be removed from office at any time through impeachment or recall.

"A Prince, whose Character is thus marked by every act which may define a Tyrant, is unfit to be the Ruler of a free People."

HOW THE KING RATED

Has he assented to wholesome laws?	No
Has he furthered Representative Government?	No
Has he dissolved Representative Houses?	Yes
Has he hindered Naturalization Laws?	Yes
Has he obstructed justice?	Yes
Is he a just ruler?	No
Is he a tyrant?	Yes

Most colonists had been forming their judgments over a long period of years. The majority of them had become convinced that the king was a "Tyrant" and that Parliament had aided him in his high-handed actions.

Today if a President, governor, or other public official assumed dictatorial powers an alert people could vote him out of office or demand that he be removed through impeachment or recall procedures. However, if the people become indifferent to their powers, this nation, like others, could fall prey to despots.

"Nor have we been wanting in Attentions to our British Brethren. We have warned them from Time to Time of Attempts by their Legislature to extend an unwarrantable Jurisdiction over us."

Let us appeal again to our British brethren. We have warned them from time to time of attempts by their legislature to extend an unwarrantable jurisdiction over us. Perhaps if we make another appeal to them they will respect our friendly but firm stand.

The Continental Congress made several direct appeals to the people of England, hoping that these appeals would

111

arouse public opinion in Britain and force Parliament to reconsider its colonial policies. After all, many generations of American colonists had lived under British rule, and for the most part, found that rule completely acceptable. Until 1776, most of the colonists simply wanted Britain to stop her oppressive acts and grant them the rights and privileges which they felt they were entitled to as British citizens.

HAD THESE EVENTS HAPPENED TODAY:

When it is necessary to appeal directly to the people of other nations today, we may do so by radio "beamed" to these nations.

> "We have reminded them of the Circumstances of our Emigration and Settlement here."

As John Bull saw it

As Jefferson saw it

Jefferson and his followers believed that the settlers who came to America acquired the lands they possessed through their own personal toil and sacrifice. Thus the allegiance they had extended to the British monarch was a voluntary one, and could be withdrawn if the king behaved like a tyrant. The British contended, however, that the Colonies were established as the result of the Crown's generosity, and therefore belonged under the king's jurisdiction. They regarded the colonists as most ungrateful subjects.

HAD THESE EVENTS HAPPENED TODAY:

"We have appealed to their native Justice and Magnanimity, and we have conjured them by the Ties of our common Kindred to disavow these Usurpations, which, would inevitably interrupt our Connections and Correspondence."

. . . the ties of our common kindred

The Colonies and the mother country had a common ancestry, language, culture, and many other mutual ties. The colonists tried in vain to appeal through these mutual interests which they shared with the British. In the statement above, Jefferson is reminding the British of this fact.

"They too have been deaf to the Voice of Justice and of Consanguinity. We must, therefore, acquiesce in the Necessity, which denounces our Separation, and hold them, as we hold the rest of Mankind, Enemies in War, in Peace Friends."

The colonists had used every kind of appeal to reason, often citing their blood relations and common ancestry as ties which the British should not regard lightly.

Today we should tell our story by radio, hoping the people of the nation to which the messages were beamed, would hear and heed.

117

"We, therefore, the Representatives of the UNITED STATES OF AMERICA, in GENERAL CONGRESS, Assembled, appealing to the Supreme Judge of the World for the Rectitude of our Intentions, do, in the Name, and by Authority of the good People of these Colonies, solemnly Publish and Declare, That these United Colonies are, and of Right ought to be, FREE AND INDEPENDENT STATES; that they are absolved from all Allegiance to the British Crown, and that all political Connection between them and the State of Great Britain, is and ought to be totally dissolved; and that as FREE AND INDEPENDENT STATES, they have full Power to levy War, conclude Peace, contract Alliances, establish Commerce, and to do all other Acts and Things which INDEPENDENT STATES may of right do."

When the "Representatives of the United States of America, in General Congress, Assembled," appealed "to the Supreme Judge of the world for the rectitude of [their] intentions, . . ." they were well aware of the seriousness and possible outcome of their acts.

History has a way of declaring successful revolutionists, heroes; unsuccessful revolutionists, traitors. With courage and provocation seldom duplicated in history, the men who wrote the Declaration, asking divine guidance in their well planned and unhurried program, undertook a course of action from which they could not withdraw.

This was no light, careless decision to make. By it they declared themselves free and independent of Britain. To the Crown and Parliament they were to have no further allegiance. They expected to be treated by the rest of the world as an independent nation subject to all the rights and responsibilities of international law.

"And for the support of this Declaration, with a firm Reliance on the Protection of divine Providence, we mutually pledge to each other our Lives, our Fortunes, and our sacred Honor."

119

These great men were proud to invoke "divine Providence" to assist them in a struggle which they realized would be long and painful. They knew that to succeed *all* must "pledge to each other our Lives, our Fortunes, and our sacred Honor." When John Hancock was asked why he signed his name to the Declaration of Independence in such large letters, he is said to have replied, "I want King George to be able to read my signature without his glasses."

It was at this time that one of the great men present at the signing is reported to have said, "Unless we hang together we shall hang separately." And this was a probability.

BIBLIOGRAPHY

Among the outstanding books on the Declaration of Independence, the five listed below are highly recommended.

Becker, Carl. *The Declaration of Independence: A Study in the History of Political Ideas.* New York: Alfred A. Knopf, 1942.

Chidsey, Donald Barr. *July, 4th, 1776—The Dramatic Story of the First Four Days of July, 1776.* New York: Crown Publishers, 1958.

Dumbauld, Edward. *The Declaration of Independence and What It Means Today.* Norman, Oklahoma: University of Oklahoma Press, 1950.

Malone, Dumas; Milhollen, Herst; and Kaplan, Milton. *The Story of the Declaration of Independence.* Toronto: Oxford University Press, 1954.

Sinclair, Merle; and McArthur, Annabel Douglas. *They Signed For Us.* New York: Duell, Sloan & Pearce, 1957.

In CONGRESS, July 4, 1776

The unanimous Declaration of the thirteen United States of America

WHEN in the Course of human Events, it becomes necessary for one People to dissolve the Political Bands which have connected them with another, and to assume among the Powers of the Earth, the separate and equal Station to which the Laws of Nature and of Nature's God entitle them, a decent Respect to the Opinions of Mankind requires that they should declare the causes which impel them to the Separation.

WE hold these Truths to be self-evident, that all Men are created equal, that they are endowed by their Creator with certain unalienable Rights, that among these are Life, Liberty, and the Pursuit of Happiness—That to secure these Rights, Governments are instituted among Men, deriving their just Powers from the Consent of the. Governed, that whenever any Form of Government becomes destructive of these Ends, it is the Right of the People to alter or to abolish it; and to institute new Government, laying its Foundation on such Principles, and organizing its Powers in such Form, as to them shall seem most likely to effect their Safety and Happiness. Prudence, indeed, will dictate that Governments long established should not be changed for light and transient Causes; and accordingly all Experience hath shewn, that Mankind are more disposed to suffer, while Evils are sufferable, than to right themselves by abolishing the

Forms to which they are accustomed. But when a long Train of Abuses and Usurpations, pursuing invariably the same Object, evinces a Design to reduce them under absolute Despotism, it is their Right, it is their Duty, to throw off such Government, and to provide new Guards for their future Security. Such has been the patient Sufferance of these Colonies; and such is now the Necessity which constrains them to alter their former Systems of Government. The History of the present King of Great-Britain is a History of repeated Injuries and Usurpations, all having in direct Object the Establishment of an absolute Tyranny over these States. To prove this, let Facts be submitted to a candid World.

HE has refused his Assent to Laws, the most wholesome and necessary for the public Good.

HE has forbidden his Governors to pass Laws of immediate and pressing Importance, unless suspended in their Operation till his Assent should be obtained; and when so suspended, he has utterly neglected to attend to them.

HE has refused to pass other Laws for the Accommodation of large Districts of People, unless those People would relinquish the Right of Representation in the Legislature, a Right inestimable to them, and formidable to Tyrants only.

HE has called together Legislative Bodies at Places unusual, uncomfortable, and distant from the Depository of their public Records, for the sole Purpose of fatiguing them into Compliance with his Measures.

HE has dissolved Representative Houses repeatedly, for opposing with manly Firmness his Invasions on the Rights of the People.

HE has refused for a long Time, after such Dissolutions, to cause others to be elected; whereby the Legislative Powers, incapable of Annihilation, have returned to the People at large for their exercise; the State remaining in the mean time exposed to all the Dangers of Invasion from without, and Convulsions within.

HE has endeavoured to prevent the Population of these States; for that Purpose obstructing the Laws for Naturalization of Foreigners; refusing to pass others to encourage their Migrations hither, and raising the Conditions of new Appropriations of Lands.

HE has obstructed the Administration of Justice, by refusing his Assent to Laws for establishing Judiciary Powers.

HE has made Judges dependent on his Will alone, for the Tenure of their Offices, and the Amount and Payment of their Salaries.

HE has erected a Multitude of new Offices, and sent hither Swarms of Officers to harrass our People, and eat out their Substance.

HE has kept among us, in Times of Peace, Standing Armies, without the consent of our Legislatures.

HE has affected to render the Military independent of and superior to the Civil Power.

HE has combined with others to subject us to a Jurisdiction foreign to our Constitution, and unacknowledged by our Laws; giving his Assent to their Acts of pretended Legislation:

FOR quartering large Bodies of Armed Troops among us:

FOR protecting them, by a mock Trial, from Punishment for any Murders which they should commit on the Inhabitants of these States:

FOR cutting off our Trade with all Parts of the World:

FOR imposing Taxes on us without our Consent:

FOR depriving us, in many Cases, of the Benefits of Trial by Jury:

FOR transporting us beyond Seas to be tried for pretended Offences:

FOR abolishing the free System of English Laws in a neighbouring Province, establishing therein an arbitrary Government, and enlarging its Boundaries, so as to render it at once an Example and fit Instrument for introducing the same absolute Rule into these Colonies:

FOR taking away our Charters, abolishing our most valuable Laws, and altering fundamentally the Forms of our Governments:

FOR suspending our own Legislatures, and declaring themselves invested with Power to legislate for us in all Cases whatsoever.

HE has abdicated Government here, by declaring us out of his Protection and waging War against us.

HE has plundered our Seas, ravaged our Coasts, burnt our Towns, and destroyed the Lives of our People.

HE is, at this Time, transporting large Armies of foreign Mercenaries to compleat the Works of Death, Desolation, and Tyranny, already begun with circumstances of Cruelty and Perfidy, scarcely paralleled in the most barbarous Ages, and totally unworthy the Head of a civilized Nation.

HE has constrained our fellow Citizens taken Captive on the high Seas to bear Arms against their Country, to become the Executioners of their Friends and Brethren, or to fall themselves by their Hands.

HE has excited domestic Insurrections amongst us, and has endeavoured to bring on the Inhabitants of our Frontiers, the merciless Indian Savages, whose known Rule of Warfare, is an undistinguished Destruction, of all Ages, Sexes and Conditions.

IN every stage of these Oppressions we have Petitioned for Redress in the most humble Terms: Our repeated Petitions have been answered only by repeated Injury. A Prince, whose Character is thus marked by every act which may define a Tyrant, is unfit to be the Ruler of a free People.

NOR have we been wanting in Attentions to our British Brethren. We have warned them from Time to Time of Attempts by their Legislature to extend an unwarrantable Jurisdiction over us. We have reminded them of the Circumstances of our Emigration and Settlement here. We have appealed to their native Justice and Magnanimity, and we have conjured them by the Ties of our common Kindred to disavow these Usurpations, which, would inevitably interrupt our Connections and Correspondence. They too have been deaf to the Voice of Justice and of Consanguinity. We must, therefore, acquiesce in the Necessity, which denounces our Separation, and hold them, as we hold the rest of Mankind, Enemies in War, in Peace, Friends.

WE, therefore, the Representatives of the UNITED STATES OF AMERICA, in GENERAL CONGRESS, Assembled, appealing to the Supreme Judge of the World for the Rectitude of our Intentions, do, in the Name, and by Authority of the good

People of these Colonies, solemnly Publish and Declare, That these United Colonies are, and of Right ought to be, FREE AND INDEPENDENT STATES; that they are absolved from all Allegiance to the British Crown, and that all political Connection between them and the State of Great-Britain, is and ought to be totally dissolved; and that as FREE AND INDEPENDENT STATES, they have full Power to levy War, conclude Peace, contract Alliances, establish Commerce, and to do all other Acts and Things which INDEPENDENT STATES may of right do. And for the support of this Declaration, with a firm Reliance on the Protection of divine Providence, we mutually pledge to each other our Lives, our Fortunes, and our sacred Honor.

John Hancock

NEW HAMPSHIRE	*Josiah Bartlett* *William Whipple* *Matthew Thornton°*
MASSACHUSETTS	*Samuel Adams* *John Adams* *Robert Treat Paine* *Elbridge Gerry*
RHODE ISLAND	*Stephen Hopkins* *William Ellery*
CONNECTICUT	*Roger Sherman* *Samuel Huntington* *William Williams* *Oliver Wolcott*
NEW YORK	*William Floyd* *Philip Livingston* *Francis Lewis* *Lewis Morris*
NEW JERSEY	*Richard Stockton* *John Witherspoon* *Francis Hopkinson* *John Hart* *Abraham Clark*

° Matthew Thornton's name was signed on the engrossed copy following the Connecticut members, but was transferred in the printed copy to its proper place with the other New Hampshire members.

PENNSYLVANIA	Robert Morris Benjamin Rush Benjamin Franklin John Morton George Clymer James Smith George Taylor James Wilson George Ross
DELAWARE	Caesar Rodney George Read Thomas Mc Kean°°
MARYLAND	Samuel Chase William Paca Thomas Stone Charles Carroll of Carrollton
VIRGINIA	George Wythe Richard Henry Lee Thomas Jefferson Benjamin Harrison Thomas Nelson, Jr. Francis Lightfoot Lee Carter Braxton
NORTH CAROLINA	William Hooper Joseph Hewes John Penn
SOUTH CAROLINA	Edward Rutledge Thomas Heyward, Jr. Thomas Lynch, Jr. Arthur Middleton
GEORGIA	Button Gwinnett Lyman Hall George Walton

°° Thomas McKean's name was not included in the original list of signers because he did not actually sign the engrossed copy until some time later, probably in 1781.